PICTURE LIBRARY

SAILING

PICTURE LIBRARY
SAILING

Norman Barrett

Franklin Watts

London   New York   Sydney   Toronto

© 1987 Franklin Watts

First published in Great Britain 1987 by
Franklin Watts
12a Golden Square
London W1R 4BA

First published in the USA by
Franklin Watts Inc
387 Park Avenue South
New York
N.Y. 10016

First published in Australia by
Franklin Watts
14 Mars Road
Lane Cove
2066 NSW

UK ISBN: 0 86313 515 3
US ISBN: 0-531-10351-X
Library of Congress Catalog Card
Number 86-51224

Printed in Italy

Designed by
Barrett & Willard

Photographs by
All-Sport
All-Sport/Duomo
All-Sport/Vandystadt
N.S. Barrett Collection
British Canoe Union

Illustration by
Rhoda & Robert Burns

Technical Consultant
James Jermain, *Yachting Monthly*

Contents

Introduction

Sailing is an international sport as well as a popular outdoor recreation. Sailing boats range from small one-person dinghies to large ocean-going yachts with a crew of twenty or more.

People enjoy sailing on lakes and reservoirs and along coasts. Some yachts are sailed across the biggest seas and oceans of the world.

△ Two-man dinghy sailing. The wind is a sailing boat's "fuel." However many crew and sails a boat has, the aim is to make the best use of the wind.

However large or small the boat, the basic principles of sailing are the same. The power of the wind, acting on the sail or sails, is used to move the boat through the water.

The wind does not have to be directly behind the boat. You can sail with the wind coming across the boat, called reaching, or into the wind at an angle, called beating, or tacking to windward.

△ A racing cruiser off the coast in calm seas. Even quite small yachts have accommodations below deck, with cooking, toilet and sleeping facilities.

The sailing boat

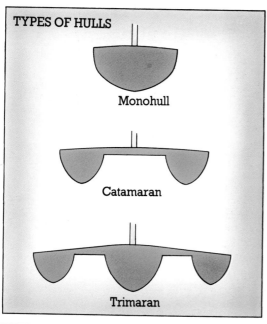

Monohull

Catamaran

Trimaran

A racing yacht of the type sailed in the America's Cup.

TACKING

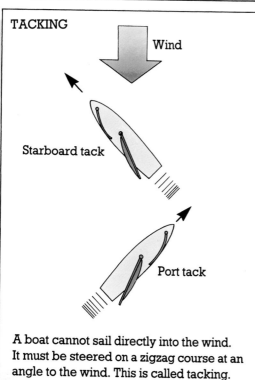

Wind

Starboard tack

Port tack

A boat cannot sail directly into the wind. It must be steered on a zigzag course at an angle to the wind. This is called tacking.

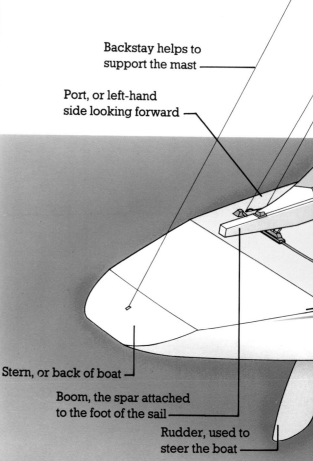

Backstay helps to support the mast

Port, or left-hand side looking forward

Stern, or back of boat

Boom, the spar attached to the foot of the sail

Rudder, used to steer the boat

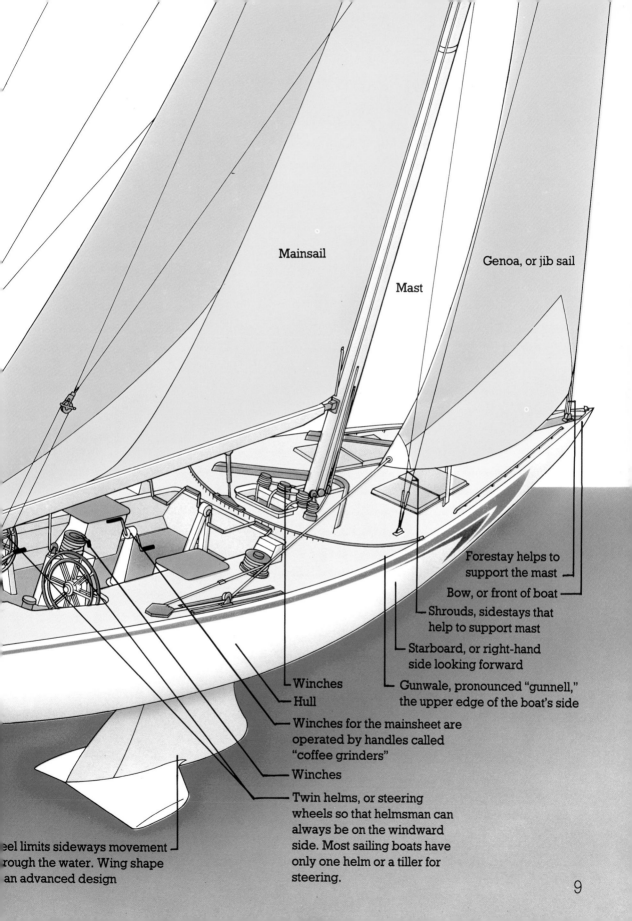

Mainsail

Mast

Genoa, or jib sail

Forestay helps to
support the mast

Bow, or front of boat

Shrouds, sidestays that
help to support mast

Starboard, or right-hand
side looking forward

Winches

Hull

Gunwale, pronounced "gunnell,"
the upper edge of the boat's side

Winches for the mainsheet are
operated by handles called
"coffee grinders"

Winches

Twin helms, or steering
wheels so that helmsman can
always be on the windward
side. Most sailing boats have
only one helm or a tiller for
steering.

eel limits sideways movement
rough the water. Wing shape
an advanced design

9

Sailing for fun

Sailing is not a dangerous sport, provided certain safety measures are taken. An approved lifejacket should be worn, and the boat should be equipped with safety gear.

A dinghy should have at least a bucket for bailing out water and a paddle for use when the wind drops. A yacht cruising off the coast may carry a life raft, flares and modern electronic aids.

△ Learning to sail in Optimist dinghies. This small but sturdy craft was designed as a training boat for youngsters, but it is also raced.

▷ Racing with spinnakers set. Spinnakers are made so that they swell out into a parachute shape. They are very powerful and are used when the wind is coming from behind.

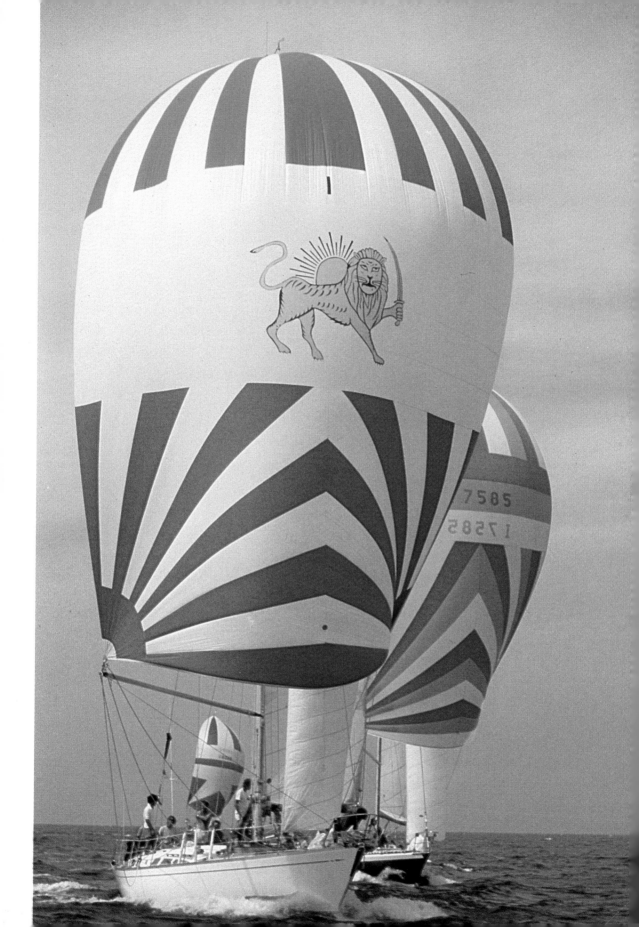

Centers where lots of boats are moored together are called marinas. The largest marinas have berths for thousands of boats. The boats may be of all shapes and sizes.

The weather at sea is changeable, and even on the hottest of days the wind can feel cold. Sailors always take warm clothing and slickers with them in case the weather changes.

▽ A jumble of boats lie at berths in a marina. Even in hot weather, sailors take warm clothes and foul-weather gear in case it turns cold and wet.

"SIGMANIA"

SIGMA

BUCKSHOT
R.O.R.C.

△ Dinghy sailing inland, on river (left) and lake. The "M" on the right-hand dinghy stands for Mirror. This is a popular class, which many people build from a kit.

▷ The Hobie Cat, a fast catamaran, or twin-hulled boat, is used for racing as well as for pleasure sailing.

Working on board

Sailing is fun, but you need to be fit. It involves hard work, whether you are sailing alone or as a member of a large crew.

Launching the boat into the water, handling the various ropes and bailing out water are just some of the things that have to be done even on the smallest dinghy.

On a large ocean-going yacht, each member of the crew has his or her own job to do.

▽ The helmsman at the steering wheel of a yacht. Another name for the tiller or wheel is the helm. So the person steering the boat is called the helmsman. In front of him can be seen the system of ropes called sheets or lines, pulleys, called blocks, and winches needed for handling the sails on a big yacht.

△ Handling the ropes
(left) and operating a
winch on a yacht.

▷ Pop star Simon Le
Bon of the Duran Duran
group checks a
computerized weather
report on his yacht
Drum. The chart table
below deck on a
modern ocean-going
yacht is equipped with
all kinds of electronic
gadgetry to aid
navigation and safe
sailing. Even so, *Drum*
capsized while
practicing for a round-
the-world race and the
crew had to be rescued.

Yacht racing

There are all kinds of classes in yacht racing. Boats of the same type race in one-design events, under rules that govern a yacht's shape and sail area. There are also handicap events for boats of different designs. The slower boats receive a time allowance.

Inshore racing takes place off the coast, on courses marked out by buoys. Offshore racing takes place across the sea or ocean.

△ The start of a yacht race. The starting line is marked by buoys, one of which can be seen on the right.

This is a one-design event for International 470s, a class of two-man dinghies. The symbol for the class, in this case "470," is displayed near the top of the mainsail.

▷ Three-man Solings racing in stormy weather. The Soling is also an international-class boat.

▷ Olympic yacht
racing: The gold-
medalists in the 470
class, Luis Doreste and
Roberto Molina of
Spain, in action during
the 1984 Games.

The two sailors are
using their weight to
balance the boat. This
must be done on small
boats when more sail is
carried to make them
go faster. The sailor on
the left is sitting on the
sidedeck, while the one
on the right is using a
trapeze. The trapeze is
a harnessed seat
suspended from high on
the mast.

△ Another race in the Los Angeles Olympics. This is a Flying Dutchman event. The Flying Dutchman is a high-performance two-man dinghy. In the center is the US boat, the eventual winner.

◁ The Tornado is a two-person catamaran, another International- and Olympic-class boat.

▷ Racing for the Admiral's Cup, an international sailing event. Each competing nation has three yachts, which race in five events, including two long offshore races.

▽ Finn dinghies round a marker buoy. These single-handers are an Olympic class, and are not easy boats to sail.

The America's Cup

The America's Cup is yacht racing's most famous trophy. Two yachts compete over a triangular course of about 25 miles (40 km) in a best of seven series of races.

The nation that holds the Cup selects a defender after a series of trials. There are also elimination trials between other nations to find a challenging yacht.

△ Yachts from the United States (top) and New Zealand competing in the 1987 America's Cup trials.

▷ *Stars and Stripes* (US) leading *Kookaburra III* (Australia) in the 1987 challenge, when the United States won back the America's Cup (insert, top left).

Long-distance racing

Some yacht races last for days or even weeks or months. There are regular transatlantic races between Britain and the United States, and also round-the-world races.

These are not just tactical races. They also test the ability and endurance of yacht and crew in all kinds of conditions. Some sailors sail the world single-handed.

▷ An entrant in the Tall Ships Race. Crews of many nationalities take part in friendly competition which provides sailing experience for hundreds of young sailors.

▽ Entrants in the Whitbread Round-the-World Race sail under Tower Bridge, London, during a publicity tour.

Other kinds of sailing

◁ Landsailing takes place on sand or pavement. The "yachts" are easy to sail, but dangerous because in a strong wind they can reach 60 mph (100 km/h) or more. The sailors, or "pilots," wear helmets and other protective clothing.

▽ Trimarans are three-hulled craft. The two outside hulls act as outriggers, or floats, to provide stability for the main, central hull.

△ Iceboats move on sharp-edged steel runners. They are even faster than land-yachts.

◁ Using the sliding seat on a sailing canoe. Sailing canoes are among the fastest of single-handed single-hulled boats. The original sporting canoes could be either sailed or paddled, but sailing canoes no longer have paddles. Canoe sailing has its own world championships.

27

The story of sailing

The first sails

Primitive man used a form of sail, probably made with animal skins, to help him propel his raft or canoe. It was only of use as a relief from paddling when the wind was blowing from behind.

For thousands of years, sailing-ships were the chief means of water transportation. But even up to the last great days of sail, in the 1800s, ships still needed a favorable wind before setting out. They could not set a course directly into the wind.

The first races

There is some evidence of yacht racing in the Netherlands in the early 1600s, but it first developed as a sport in England in the later 1600s, during the reign of King Charles II. The first race took place in 1661 along the River Thames, between the yachts of King Charles and the Duke of York. The sport continued as a pastime for the wealthy, with match races between two or more yachts for huge wagers.

The America's Cup

In 1851, the schooner *America* crossed the Atlantic to take on the best of British yachts. It beat the opposition hands down, and in memory of this famous victory the permanent challenge trophy which it won has been called the America's Cup ever since.

△ The US schooner *America*, which beat the best of British yachts in 1851.

The great clipper race

In the late 1800s, the great clipper ships that carried tea from China to England raced to see who could bring the first of the

△ The *Taeping* and the *Ariel* on the high seas during the great clipper race of 1866.

season's crop to market. The tea importers in London offered a prize for the first ship home. In the exciting 1866 race, nine ships took part, and after nearly 100 days' sailing, the *Taeping* beat the *Ariel* by a mere 20 minutes.

Iceboating

Iceboating caught on as a sport in the United States in the 1860s. It was an iceboat that first traveled at 100 mph (160 km/h), before the days of the automobile and the airplane.

△ Iceboating on the Delaware River, in 1885.

Olympic yacht racing

Yacht racing as we know it today began to develop around the beginning of this century. But yachts were the toys of the rich, sailed with large crews of paid hands. The first Olympic yachting events were held in 1900, with yachts ranging from ½ ton to 20 tons in size.

In the 1920s, smaller boats began to be raced, and a wide range of classes competed in the Olympics.

△ A sailing event in the 1984 Olympics, off the US west coast.

A popular sport

In the late 1940s, people started building their own dinghies from kits. The boom in the sport was due to the development of marine plywood and special glues during World War II (1939–45). The later development of fibreglass as a material for yachts also reduced the costs of boat-building. So what was once just a sport of kings is now a sport for everyone.

Facts and records

△ A bird's-eye view of *Australia II*.

Long-playing record

The longest unbeaten record in all of sport was held by the United States in the America's Cup. The trophy, won by the yacht *America* in 1851, remained in the New York Yacht Club for 132 years, during which time 24 challenges were beaten off. Finally, in 1983, the Australian yacht *Australia II* took the Cup out of the United States.

△ The record-breaking *Crossbow II*.

The fastest

The official world speed record,

measured on a 547 yd (500 m) course, was set by the British yacht *Crossbow II* in 1980. Steered by its owner Timothy Colman, it recorded a speed of 36.04 knots (41.5 mph or 67 km/h). This has since been beaten by windsurfers.

Super

One of the most successful racing dinghies of all time was as famous for its name as it was for its exploits. It was called *Supercalifragilistichexpialidocious*, or *Superdocious* for short. In the 1968 Olympic Games, with Rodney Pattisson of Great Britain at the helm, *Superdocious* won the Flying Dutchman gold medal and dominated the class for years. Pattisson went on to win the gold again at the 1972 Games in the slightly shorter named *Superdoso*.

△ *Superdoso*—its full name may be seen on the side of the hull.

Glossary

Beating
Sailing to windward by taking a zigzag course, or tacking.

Bow
The front of the boat.

Catamaran
A twin-hulled boat.

Dinghy
A small sailing boat, without a cabin below deck.

Helm
The steering gear.

Inshore racing
Racing off the coast.

Keel
Fin that prevents boat slipping sideways in the water.

Offshore racing
Racing across the sea.

Reaching
Sailing with the wind coming from the side.

Rudder
Blade under the boat's hull that is used for steering.

Sheet
Rope used to control a sail.

Shroud
Sidestay for the mast.

Spinnaker
A billowy sail used to make a boat sail faster with the wind.

Stay
Support for the mast.

Stern
The back of the boat.

Tacking
Sailing a zigzag course toward the direction of the wind.

Tiller
A handle connected to the top of the rudder and used for steering.

Trimaran
A three-hulled boat.

Winch
A device for winding ropes in and out.

Windward
Where the wind is coming from.

Index